OFFICE OF INDIAN AFFAIRS

SOME THINGS THAT GIRLS SHOULD KNOW HOW TO DO

AND HENCE SHOULD LEARN HOW TO DO WHEN IN SCHOOL

WASHINGTON
GOVERNMENT PRINTING OFFICE
1911

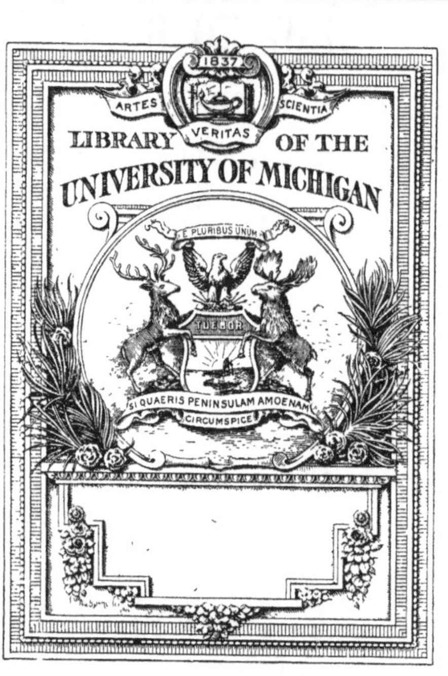
1837
ARTES
SCIENTIA
VERITAS
LIBRARY OF THE
UNIVERSITY OF MICHIGAN
E PLURIBUS UNUM
TUEBOR
SI QUAERIS PENINSULAM AMOENAM
CIRCUMSPICE

CONTENTS.

PREFACE.

This publication has been compiled from the results of practical experience in the work of instruction in the Indian schools. It is believed that it is a comprehensive and practical manual that will be of material assistance to the teacher, but every teacher is urged to forward suggestions in order that the manual may be improved when a second edition is issued.

One word of caution is urged as to the use of this publication. The teachers should look at it in the light of suggestions rather than as dogma from which they should never deviate, and I should not want any teachers to feel that they could not take up any phases of the subject or any methods of instruction which are not contained in this publication. Conditions vary greatly in different localities and in the same locality at different times, and the teacher must ever be alert to meet these changes. Perhaps this word of caution is unnecessary, but the experience of many school systems goes to show that it can not be too strongly emphasized.

R. G. VALENTINE, *Commissioner*.

SOME THINGS THAT GIRLS SHOULD KNOW HOW TO DO.

INTRODUCTION.

Instruction, according to the outline which follows, is to be given where it is presumed that the pupil will not go out to work but will return home after finishing the day or reservation boarding school course. It would be well to give actual practice in the homes of some of the people with the assistance of the field matron. There are many old and helpless Indians on reservations who would not resent being assisted in this way. The girls would receive actual experience under difficulties which confront the average Indian and which distress the educated student upon his return from a different mode of life in the boarding school. Avoid large classes. Spend much of your energy upon striving for excellence in training instead of trying to maintain discipline with larger numbers.

In order to have the persons who are before you interested in the work you must be thoroughly interested yourself. To command interest there must be the right attitude toward the thing required, the people who require it, and for whom it is required.

The real Indian pupil must grow naturally into the habit of performing the task put before him. He must feel the need of and perform the task many times before he can do it independently from his own initiative.

Have the pupils make drawings and illustrations in their notebooks so that they will have a mechanical as well as a verbal understanding of the lesson given.

Give them frequent opportunities for invention. Lead them to do of their own volition when you can, instead of slavishly copying every act of yours.

Give actual with verbal experience as often as possible. With many classes you will find that the illustration and demonstration will have to precede the explanation.

Give tests in the comparison of goods of different qualities so that power of discrimination in values may be attained. Give experiences in the terms and expressions used in buying and selling. Teach the girl how not to pay $36 for a $22.50 tailored suit.

Sample record card (face).

Name........................ Age......... Tribe........................
Date of entry................. Term....... Grade in school...............

Article.	Date.	Process.	Date.	Remarks.
	1907.		1907.	
1	Sept. 25	16	Nov. 5	
			1908.	
2	Oct. 1	12	Jan. 4	
3	Oct. 15	13	Jan. 4	
5	Oct. 20	1	Mar. 11	
14	Nov. 1	2	Apr. 5	
6	Nov. 15	15	June 15	
4	Nov. 24	17	Oct. 13	
32	Dec. 15	18	Oct. 13	
	1908.		1909.	
8	Feb. 5	10	Jan. 9	
9	May 17	5	Feb. 15	
22	May 31	3	May 20	
10	Oct. 11	4	June 15	
12	Nov. 19	6	Oct. 30	
15	Dec. 22	7	Oct. 30	
	1909.		1910.	
11	Jan. 13	11	June 15	
17	Mar. 27	14	June 16	
20	May 7	20	June 15	
21	June 15			
19	Oct. 16			
24	Nov. 21			
	1910.			
27	Jan. 29			
25	Mar. 19			
31	May 11			
33	June 15			
28	June 15			

Sample record card (reverse).

This card is to be used in recording the work done by each girl during her attendance in school. All of the articles mentioned may not be applicable to each individual, and it may be desirable to teach other processes and the making of other articles in different localities, but whenever anything is made that is not in the list, or when anything practicable is taught that is not found there, these should be inserted with appropriate number and the proper credit given.

ARTICLES TO BE MADE.

1. Sewing bag.
2. Needlebook.
3. Apron.
4. Laundry bag.
5. Iron holder.
6. Towel.
7. Pincushion.
8. Sheet.
9. Pillow cover.
10. Bedtick.
11. Mattress cover.
12. Curtain.
13. Screen.
14. Dish towel.
15. Napkin.
16. Bureau scarf.
17. Tablecloth.
18. Baby's dress.
19. Child's dress.
20. Girl's dress.
21. Boy's waist.
22. Boy's suspenders.
23. Boy's trousers.
24. Shirt waist.
25. Dress.
26. Shirt.
27. Skirt.
28. Embroidered doily
29. Centerpiece.
30. Sofa-pillow cover.
31. Handkerchief.
32. Shoe bag.
33. Underwear.

PROCESSES TO BE LEARNED.

1. Bread making.
2. Baking.
3. Cooking meat.
4. Cooking vegetables.
5. Making cake.
6. Drying fruit.
7. Making pickles.
8. Making candy.
9. Milking.
10. Making butter.
11. Sewing.
12. Mending.
13. Darning.
14. Cutting and fitting.
15. Laundering.
16. Cleaning.
17. Dry cleaning.
18. Pressing.
19. Embroidering.
20. Nursing.

SUGGESTIONS IN EQUIPMENT.

[To give pupils an idea of what is required in plain home furnishings.]

Estimated cost of equipment.

KITCHEN.

2 bowls, pint, at 20 cents each	$0.40
2 bowls, quart, at 25 cents each	.50
1 bowl, chopping, at 25 cents	.25
1 bowl, butter, at 50 cents	.50
1 boiler, double oatmeal, at 50 cents	.50
2 crocks, 1 gallon, at 20 cents each	.40
1 crock, 2 gallon, at 30 cents	.30
1 crock, 3 gallon, at 40 cents	.40
1 cake box, tin, at 40 cents	.40
1 cabinet, kitchen, at $12	12.00
1 churn, at $1	1.00
1 cutter, biscuit and cooky, at 5 cents	.05
1 knife, chopping, at 25 cents	.25
1 knife, butcher, at 15 cents	.15
1 kettle, enamel, large, at 50 cents	.50
1 kettle, enamel, small, at 40 cents	.40
1 grater, large, at 20 cents	.20
1 nutmeg grater, at 10 cents	.10
1 grinder, meat, at $1.50	1.50
1 griddle, pancake, at 75 cents	.75
1 colander, at 20 cents	.20
1 kettle, iron, at 60 cents	.60
1 ladle, butter, at 10 cents	.10
24 jars, glass, fruit, 1 quart, at $1.40 per dozen	2.80
3 jugs, 1 gallon, at 10 cents each	.30
1 mill, coffee, at 25 cents	.25
1 masher, potato, at 15 cents	.15
1 pan, cake, at 10 cents	.10
2 pans, bread, at 20 cents each	.40
1 muffin pan, at 50 cents	.50
2 pans, stew, enamel, 1 pint, at 25 cents each	.50
1 pan, stew, enamel, 1 quart, at 40 cents	.40
3 pans, milk, at 25 cents each	.75
1 pan, frying, at 20 cents	.20
1 pan, dust, at 25 cents	.25
2 pans, dish, at 50 cents each	1.00

1 pin, rolling, at 20 cents	$0.20
6 plates, pie, tin, at 10 cents each	.60
1 pot, tea, at 50 cents	.50
1 pot, coffee, at 50 cents	.50
2 spoons, basting, at 5 cents each	.10
6 spoons, table, at 8 cents each	.48
12 spoons, tea, at 4 cents each	.48
1 strainer, milk, at 25 cents	.25
1 steamer, at 30 cents	.30
1 sifter, flour, at 20 cents	.20
1 skimmer, at 10 cents	.10
1 table, kitchen, at $2	2.00
1 turner, pancake, at 10 cents	.10
1 toaster, at 20 cents	.20
1 tray, at 10 cents	.10
2 pitchers, enamel, 1 quart, at 40 cents each	.80
1 waffle iron, at $1.50	1.50
1 cook stove, small, at $10	10.00
1 set knives and forks (steel), at $1	1.00
12 tumblers, at 10 cents each	1.20
1 set of dishes, at $10	10.00
1 closet for dishes, at $5	5.00
1 boiler, wash, at 80 cents	.80
1 machine, washing, at $6	6.00
2 irons, sad, 6 pound, at 20 cents each	.40
2 irons, sad, 7 pound, at 25 cents each	.50
1 iron, sad, 8 pound, at 30 cents	.30
1 ironing board, at $1	1.00
1 clothes rack, at 75 cents	.75
1 clothes basket, at $1	1.00
1 ironing stand, at 10 cents	.10
1 whisk broom, at 10 cents	.10
1 sleeve board, at 50 cents	.50
1 washing board, at 40 cents	.40
2 tubs, at 75 cents each	1.50
1 wringer, at $3.50	3.50
1 dipper, at 10 cents	.10
1 kettle, at 50 cents	.50
1 ironing sheet, at 20 cents	.20
1 holder, at 10 cents	.10

SITTING ROOM (USED ALSO FOR DINING ROOM).

1 table, at $10	10.00
6 chairs, at $1.50 each	9.00
1 rocking chair, at $3	3.00
Rugs (home made).	
1 lamp, at $1.50	1.50
1 organ, at $35	35.00
1 clock, at $3	3.00
1 couch, at $10	10.00
1 couch cover, at $1.50	1.50
Curtains (home made).	

BEDROOM.

1 bedstead, double, at $8	$8.00
1 bureau with glass, at $10	10.00
1 sewing machine, at $20	20.00
1 mattress, single, at $3	3.00
1 mattress, double, at $4	4.00
1 bedstead, single, at $6	6.00
1 washstand, at $6	6.00
1 screen (home made).	
1 lamp, at 75 cents	.75

MISCELLANEOUS.

1 bucket, water, at 50 cents	.50
1 mopstick, at 25 cents	.25
1 scrub brush, at 15 cents	.15
1 hammer, at 50 cents	.50
1 screw-driver, at 25 cents	.25
1 saw, at $1.10	1.10
1 ax, at 95 cents	.95
100 feet of clothesline, at 50 cents	.50
Total	217.36

OUTLINE LESSONS.

EQUIPMENT OF KITCHEN AND PREPARATION OF FOOD.

LESSON I.

The equipment of an ordinary kitchen: List of articles needed for same, with prices. Look for these articles in illustrated catalogues. Find prices. Find country-store prices. Have pupils make lists in notebooks of such articles as the average Indian of the community will buy and use.

LESSON II.

Food supplies for ordinary home: List of these, with prices. How to store supplies when living in a one-room house. Rough shelves and boxes nailed to the walls. How to arrange these and where to get them. The outside shed for storing things. Teach the desirability of a larger house. Do not be satisfied with one room.

LESSON III.

The cellar: Props and excavation. Country people and farmers use cellars for storing vegetables and fruit. Care of cellar. How the Navajos keep their supplies. How squirrels, woodpeckers, beavers, wood rats, etc., store their food. Stories of people of other lands. The Eskimo house.

64631°—11——2

LESSON IV.

The stove: Different kinds of stoves; the kind to select for an Indian home. Price, where to buy, and how much to pay. Look for stoves in catalogues. The Dutch oven for camping. Its use and advantage over the camp fire.

LESSON V.

How to build fires: Explain the use of dampers, oven, ash pan, etc. Fires of wood and coal. Providing kindling and wood. Price of fuel. How to economize with fire. How much fuel to buy. Care of the stove. Kind of polish; how used. How much to pay and what to ask for. Experience in buying. How to construct a rough shelter for wood in wet countries.

LESSON VI.

The kitchen table: How to make a log table when camping. How to make a rough board table. (See Farm and Home Mechanics.)

LESSON VII.

How to make benches from rough boards. (See Farm and Home Mechanics.) Bread boards, bread boxes, rolling pins, etc.

LESSON VIII.

Care of the table: List of dishes for a family. Prices, names, etc. How to buy and what to pay.

LESSON IX.

Oilcloth for tables: Oilcloth used in some country homes; different kinds of oilcloth. Prices, and how much to buy. Better than eating from the table. White tablecloth better than oilcloth.

LESSON X.

Cupboards: The use of boxes and rough boards in making. Oilcloth and newspapers for the shelves. Curtains for doors. Arrangement of dishes. Small box for knives and forks. How to make, with handle.

LESSON XI.

Dish washing: Use of soap and water. Hot water for washing dishes. Put the water on to warm during the meal time. Make wash cloths and towels from flour sacks. (See sewing outline.) Soapy water, rinse water; economize in use of soap. Place to keep soap; can with nail holes.

LESSON XII.

Yeast: How to make. Place to keep it. Recipe and practice in making. How to buy and price. If practical, tell something about growth of yeast.

LESSON XIII.

Flour: Different brands, what to pay, and place to keep. Make a flour box with cover. Make a cover for flour barrel. (See Farm and Home Mechanics.)

LESSON XIV.

Bread: How to make. Proportions of flour, salt, yeast, to use. Measuring by cups, teaspoons, tablespoons, pinches; practice in making bread. Recipe.

LESSON XV.

How to make dinner rolls: Practice in making. Practice in making different shaped loaves, cinnamon rolls, coffee cake, etc. Clean bread boxes to have ready for bread when baked. Tell why it is best not to put bread in covered receptacle while fresh from the oven.

LESSON XVI.

How to use the oven in baking: How to use soda, cream of tartar, and baking powder. Recipe for baking-powder biscuit. Practice in making.

LESSON XVII.

Corn meal: How the Indians grind. How much to buy for family and the cost. How to make corn bread. Recipe. Practice in making.

LESSON XVIII.

Corn-meal muffins: How to make. Proportions of ingredients. Recipe.

LESSON XIX.

How to make griddle cakes and pan bread. Tortilla. Tell about Navajo and Pueblo bread making.

LESSON XX.

Oatmeal: How to buy in tin cans. Where to keep from weevil. Proportions for each person. How to cook. Double boiler. How to use. Price. Recipe.

LESSON XXI.

The use of lard and butter: Saving fats of meats. Bacon, pork, etc. Doughnuts. How to make. Recipe.

LESSON XXII.

Meat, beefsteak: How to select. How to weigh. The amount to buy for a family. Price. Where to keep from flies. Experience in calculation. Prepare and broil steak. How to broil over the stove. How to broil in camp. Recipe.

LESSON XXIII.

Fried steak: Fried steak with onions. Practice.

LESSON XXIV.

How to select roast meat: Amount to buy. Price to pay. Prepare and roast. Recipe. Price. Make brown gravy.

LESSON XXV.

Stewed beef: Selection. What price to pay. How to make dumplings. Recipe.

LESSON XXVI.

Use of meats in making soup: Use of rice and vegetables in soup. Make beef soup. Vegetable soup. Tomato soup. Chicken broth. Noodle soup, etc.

LESSON XXVII.

Potatoes: How to pare. Boil. Place to keep potatoes. Price per bushel or pound. Use of left-over boiled potatoes. Practice in boiling. Experience in buying and selling.

LESSON XXVIII.

Fried potatoes: Prepare and fry. How to boil first and then fry. Economy in lard. Onions fried, boiled. Use in fried potatoes. Pickled onions.

LESSON XXIX.

Beans: Baked beans. Clean, soak. How to measure. How to buy and sell by the bushel. How to bake with sliced pork.

LESSON XXX.

Chops: How to select. Price. Broiled or fried. Pork and mutton chops. Breaded chops, etc.

LESSON XXXI.

The different kinds of fish: How to prepare. How to dry, fry, bake. How to salt fish to keep. Where to keep it.

LESSON XXXII.

Prepare boiled beans: Lesson on lima beans. Navy beans. Frijoles. Place to store beans.

LESSON XXXIII.

How to cook: Cabbage, cauliflower, squash, baked, fried, and boiled. Turnips, tomatoes, greens, and onions.

LESSON XXXIV.

Tea: How to buy. Cost. Place to keep it so that the flavor will not be lost. Care of the teapot. Hot water for tea. Pouring off the grounds before absorption of tannin. Not good for babies or young children. Make and serve. Recipe.

LESSON XXXV.

Plain cake with eggs: How to beat eggs. How to make cake without eggs. Measuring by cups, teaspoons, tablespoons. Make cakes and serve.

LESSON XXXVI.

How to make molasses cake and cookies. Recipe. Make and serve.

LESSON XXXVII.

Pie: How to make crust. How to stew fruit. Amounts to use. Recipe for crust. Practice in making.

LESSON XXXVIII.

Dried fruit: Names. Prices. How to buy. How to dry and care for. Where to keep.

LESSON XXXIX.

Fresh fruit: How to stew, pickle, and can. How to make jelly. Keep canned fruit in cellar. How to buy and sell. Prices. Notes and recipes.

LESSON XL.

How to pickle cucumbers, watermelon rinds, etc.

LESSON XLI.

How to make simple candies.

ADDITIONAL SUGGESTIONS.

From time to time prepare simple meals and serve them. Teachers are at liberty to enlarge upon the lessons at any time that better ideas occur to them.

Give many practice lessons. Have enough variety so that the work will progress with interest, and above all arouse in the pupil a desire to learn. Give exhibitions of work frequently by way of encouragement.

Make a collection of talks and stories to intersperse between your exercises. The Indian is very fond of a good story. He has great regard for the person who is capable of doing the right thing in the right way at the right time.

Do not force the work upon the pupil, but arouse in him the desire to accept what you have to give. The gift and the acceptance will naturally follow.

Teach pupils what you know about the correct way of eating, having them put this knowledge into practice when meals are served to classes.

Review the lessons often. You can not expect results unless the lesson given "sinks in" deep enough to come out in expression.

Give the instruction as outlined, but do not be content with that if it is in your power to give more.

In the selection of supplies, and experience in buying and selling, the classes may be benefited by trips to the country store and to the commissary.

In places where supplies and furnishings are issued to Indians the pupils may spend a day profitably with the field matron arranging them in an Indian home. They will enjoy this, and if tactfully managed the Indians will be grateful. Good use may be made of the boxes in which goods are shipped to the different schools in making simple furnishings for Indian homes.

CARE AND EQUIPMENT OF BEDROOMS.

LESSON I.

Care of beds and bedding: Care of bed clothing where people sleep on the ground or floor. Make a covered camp bed with folded blankets or quilts.

LESSON II.

Show how to make corn husk or straw mattresses with one or two buttoned openings: Demonstrate. Pupil's notes.

LESSON III.

Make bedticks to fill with pine needles, leaves, etc.: Price and kinds of material to buy for corn husk or straw mattresses. The advantage of washable covers for mattresses where sheets are not used and water is scarce for use in the care of white clothes. Care of blankets. How to wash in the snow. What to buy to soften the water when washing blankets. How much to use. Demonstrate washing blankets.

LESSON IV.

How to make corn husk or straw pillows, and colored covers for same: Prices. What to ask for and how much to buy. Experience in buying where practicable.

LESSON V.

The making of curtains or screens for beds to be used at night: The beginning of privacy, where several persons or families sleep in the one room. What to use, how to secure it, and what to pay for it. Experience in estimation. Calculation and purchase. Pupils' notes. (See Farm and Home Mechanics for screen frames.)

LESSON VI.

Making simple clothes boxes of a size small enough to be pushed under the beds in houses where the room space is at a premium: These boxes may be covered with paper or cloth, plain or fancy, as desired. Soap, starch, and fruit boxes from the stores or trading posts lend themselves well for this work. Shoe boxes may be made to match.

LESSON VII.

How to make bureau from a dry goods box: Making shelves, curtains, top cover, etc. How to make washstands from dry goods boxes. Shelves, curtain, oilcloth cover, etc., for same.

LESSON VIII.

How to make simple folding beds for the one-room house: How to make hammock beds with old bed springs for out of doors. How to make table beds for out of doors, where there are trees.

Care of bedding, mattress slips of muslin or other material, which can be washed and with which the matress can be covered when camping.

HOUSEKEEPING SUGGESTIONS.

LESSON I.

How to care systematically for household articles when living a nomadic life: A place to put supplies. A place to put clothing. A place to put bedding. How to wash and keep things clean. The use of plenty of good soap. The contented housekeeper.

LESSON II.

The necessity for system in cramped quarters: The necessity for absolute cleanliness. Fixing a rack for bedding. Camping materials and outfits which can be purchased from local dealers or by catalogue. Suitable camp equipment. The hammock bed. The basket dish outfit. The Dutch oven and its use, etc. The simple metal washstand, the cot bed, etc. The tent. (For Indians in sections of the country who will live in tents and have the money which will be spent in other ways if not in this way.)

LESSON III.

The trunk or box for clothes: Make box moth and bug proof. Line with paper or cloth. Show how to arrange and keep clean. Bags for soiled clothes. Keep separate from clean clothes. Bags and suitable coverings for everything used which should be protected. How to make a small screen box for meat to hang in the trees.

LESSON IV.

The water bottle, canteens: Price. Care of water, and its treatment for drinking purposes. Use of oatmeal in water. Treatment of water for purifying. What to use. Experience in boiling and cooling. Stories from Mary Austin's Land of Little Rain. The Trail in the Desert where the animals came down to the water holes at night.

LESSON V.

Selection of material for clothing where it is inconvenient to laundry: Names of samples and prices. Where to buy. How to ask for same, practice in English terms. This list varies in different communities.

LESSON VI.

Review commercial English: How to keep from paying too much for articles purchased. Correct prices of ribbon, silk, velvet, velveteens, etc.

CLEANING.

LESSON I.

Floors: How to sweep. What to put on the floor to keep the dust from flying. Germs carried in dust.

Demonstrate: When to dust after sweeping. Where to keep the broom, dust pan, and the dust rag in the one-room house. Have a barrel or stand. What brooms and dustpans cost. The story of Cinderella.

LESSON II.

How to scrub the floor: Use of soap, scrub brush, and lye. Cost of each. What to ask for when buying and how to do it. How to make a mop from an old broom. How to scrub clean with an old broom. How often to clean the home floor. Make mental calculations on change if certain amounts are paid.

LESSON III.

How to keep an adobe floor clean. How to hang things from the rafters in an adobe house.

LESSON IV.

Painted floors: What colors are best. (Where there are field matrons the class may go to some home to get this work to do.) Prices of paint. What to get and how much. What price should be paid. Mental calculations. Experience in buying.

LESSON V.

Requisites for painting: The brush, the tin or guard to keep from spattering. How to mix. Pupils practice in painting. (See Farm and Home Mechanics.)

LESSON VI.

Care of the walls: Use of newspapers. How to put up simple rough board shelves. How to cover with newspapers. A shelf for the clock. A shelf for trinkets. How to make paper racks. Where to get nails, what sizes. How much to pay for nails and tacks. How to use a stone or stick where there is no hammer. Price. Pupils practice making shelves. Notes.

LESSON VII.

How to hang paper if it is desired to paper the little rooms in a home. Have pupils make cardboard walls papered with wall paper, showing how to match, trim, and paste. Show how to make paste. Recipe. Notes.

LESSON VIII.

How to whiten walls with lime. How to mix lime whitewash. Price. What kind of brush to use. Price. How much lime to buy and what to pay for it. (See Farm and Home Mechanics.) Kind of brush and price. How lime is purifying in its action. Its use as a disinfectant.

Demonstration. Pupils' notes. Exercises in English. How to ask for articles. What change to make, etc.

LESSON IX.

Ornamentation of a simple home: The use of beadwork, baskets, pottery, skins, ornamented skins, bows and arrows. Shelves for pottery if the home is in the Southwest. Ornamentation with blankets if in the Navajo country. Bows and arrows, beadwork, and skins if in the North.

Poster pictures, pictures from magazines, calendars, etc., if in the Southeast and in many of the homes of the Plains Indians.

LESSON X.

Rug making and carpet weaving: Different kinds of rugs. Navajo rugs. Patch rugs with buttonhole border. Drawn rugs, etc. Rugs of corduroy. Carpet from grain sacks.

LESSON XI.

Making screens and curtains: The willow and beadwork screen for keeping out flies. Screening windows and doors. The window screen. Country people often buy by the yard and tack it on without frames. How to buy by the yard. How much to buy for ordinary window. How to fasten with strips, etc.

LESSON XII.

How to make screen frames. Demonstrate. (See Farm and Home Mechanics.) Screen doors. Where to buy, how much to pay.

LESSON XIII.

The advantage of screens. The danger of contagion from flies and mosquitoes.

SEWING.

LESSON I.

Sewing equipment: Sewing bags, needles, thimbles, scissors, thread, etc. Making sewing bags. Teach stitches of different kinds. Have samplers for stitching. (See Kirkwood's School Sewing.) Making sewing bags.

LESSON II.

Hemming towels: Towels made of flour sacks to be used in wiping dishes. Sew strips to be attached to flour sacks as a fastening to close and hang up with articles in, when camping.

LESSON III.

How to make plain colored aprons. Price of goods and how much to ask for when buying. What is best in apron goods.

LESSON IV.

Making simple curtains. Making pillow covers. Making sheets. Practice in stitching. Care and use of the machine. Mending stockings. Mending aprons, dresses, men's and boys' clothing.

LESSON V.

Making aprons, towels, etc., on the machine.

LESSON VI.

How to make little children's clothes. Baby dresses, bands, bibs, sack aprons, underwear, etc. Selection of material. Price of same. How to select ready-made clothing. Where to buy and the cost. Show samples. How to buy men's ready-made clothing. Prices. How to buy children's clothing. How to buy women's ready-made clothing.

LESSON VII.

How to cut underskirt from pattern. What material to get. Price. How to buy ready made. Price. Where to get patterns. How to ask for by number. Where to send for. Price.

LESSON VIII.

How to cut, baste, and sew plain skirt. Material, percales, etc. Prices.

LESSON IX.

How to make simple waist. Cut from pattern. Make bag for patterns.

LESSON X.

How to make boys' waists. Pattern for same. Selection of materials. Price.

LESSON XI.

How to make men's shirts from pattern: Selection of material. What to select and how much to pay. Study of materials from samples. Notes.

LESSON XII.

Teach the advantage of having a change of clothing for babies, children, and grown people.

LESSON XIII.

Make list of clothing with approximate prices for a family. Review how to make, buy ready-made, etc.

LAUNDERING.

LESSON I.

What is needed for washing: List of articles such as the Indian can afford and will use. How to manage with one washtub. Soap and its use. How to buy. How much to pay. How to soften the water. Soaking clothes over night, boiling before rubbing, and vice versa. Find illustrations of each. article, with price. Teach pupils how to purchase these articles, how to ask for them in English, and what amount to pay. Experience. Pupils' notes. Putting up the clothes line; attaching to trees, to the house; putting down posts for same.

LESSON II.

Demonstration in washing: Teach the great mission of the cake of soap and boiling water. How to make a good soapsuds. Difference between good and poor washing. How to make starch. How to make bluing. Arrangement of clothes on line. Bringing in at night. Advantage of the big iron kettle for washing and cleaning. How to hang. Price of same. Where to buy. Place to keep tub, washboard, etc.

LESSON III.

Talks on kinds of clothes that do not appear to bad advantage if not ironed. How to fold and press clothes where it is not possible to iron, as in camp life. Dampening and folding. Demonstration in ironing. Pupils' notes.

LESSON IV.

Dry cleaning "the Navajo velveteen shirt," blankets. How to clean blankets with corn meal or damp salt. The use of the brush and whisk broom in cleaning where there is a scarcity of water.

LESSON V.

The use of ammonia in water: How to secure and what price to pay. Cleaning woolens with snow.

LESSON VI.

Cleaning men's clothing with a small amount of water, soap, and a whisk broom or with a bundle of straw or pine needles. A corn cob lends itself also for this purpose.

LESSON VII.

Dry cleaning under suitable conditions: Pressing and cleaning woolen clothes.

LESSON VIII.

(Give much practice in the details of each lesson, reviewing often enough to give the learner the faculty to do the thing independently.)

LESSON IX.

Personal cleanliness: List of articles for same. Wash basin; towel; towel rack, string, or nail; comb, brush, and place to keep. Toilet soap: ivory, castile, etc. Where to buy. How much to pay. The small square towel to be used by one person once.

LESSON X.

Care of the hair for cleanliness: The fine comb. The day's routine of cleanliness. The bath or oil cleaning at least once a week. How to make a small amount of soapy water serve the purpose.

DAIRYING.

LESSON I.

How to milk the cow and care for her: Place to keep her. What time she should be milked. Why the same person should milk the cow each time if possible. Care of milk pans, strainer, etc. Practice in cleaning.

LESSON II.

What utensils to buy for the care of milk, milk pans, strainers, etc. Where to keep in the one or two room house or the camp. Price of each. Pupils' notes.

LESSON III.

How to set milk in a tub or bucket of water. How to keep cool with clean damp cloths. How and when to skim. Where to keep cream for butter making. Where and when to churn.

LESSON IV.

Buying a churn: Where to buy. What size to get. What price to pay. Care of the churn. How to churn cream. Use of the dasher churn. Use of the revolving churn. Difference in price. Which would be most convenient for a simple home. How to make butter. Practice.

LESSON V.

Milk for young children: Teaching them to like it. Goats' milk for children. Care of same. Richer than cows' milk.

LESSON VI.

Condensed milk: How to buy. How to dilute. How to give to young children and babies. Use for sick persons.

LESSON VII.

The use of milk in cooking. The use of milk in feeding pigs and chickens. Use of buttermilk. Learning to drink it.

LESSON VIII.

Use of sour milk. Making cottage cheese.

CARE OF SICK.

LESSON I.

Care of the sick: Isolation; cleanliness. What remedies to keep at home. How to use them. The use of simple emetics. Simple remedies to give when a cold is coming on. How to make onion sirup for coughs. What to do for croup.

LESSON II.

Care of the eyes of babies and children. Necessity for cleanliness. The use of eye washes. How to make a simple boracic eye wash. How to use it. How much to buy and the price.

LESSON III.

The advantage of following the doctor's advice. Local examples. Visiting the sick. Doing informal acts of kindness.

LESSON IV.

What kind of food to give the sick. Toast, soups, milk, etc. How to take care of sick in camp. Having a change of clothes. Buying white cheese cloth for cloths, etc.; easily washed. How to keep well. Plenty of fresh air.

LESSON V.

Exercise, work, good temper, care in eating. Cleanliness. Ventilation; keeping the windows open. Avoiding the use of canned goods. How simple eating is best. How the Indians were better in the days when they did not use so many canned meats and sweets, etc. Tell stories of great endurance.

LESSON VI.

More economical to have simple foods. Explain the difference in cost of goods in bulk and in cans.

LESSON VII.

Give tension, breathing, and other exercises for the strengthening of all parts of the body.

CARE OF CAMP ANIMALS.

LESSON I.

The dog: How the poor man is known by the number of dogs he has. How many dogs to keep. The value of one good watchdog. The disadvantage of having so many dogs where there are no herds to take care of and food is scarce. How to care for one good dog. Box for sleeping, instead of sleeping with the family. Dish for feeding, etc. Pupils' notes. Tell stories of dogs.

LESSON II.

Care of pueblo and camp chickens: Rough shelter for same. How to protect from wild-cat, fox, weasel, coyote; when to feed. Saving scraps and milk. Care of the eggs. Making nests with boxes, using straw, leaves, excelsior, etc. Setting hens and caring for them. Demonstrate—making nests. Pupils' notes.

LESSON III.

Care of little chickens: What to feed them. Protection from lice. How to protect at night. Making rough shelters with boxes. Setting traps for vermin, etc. What to pay for traps and where to get them.

O

www.ingramcontent.com/pod-product-compliance
Lightning Source LLC
LaVergne TN
LVHW012330100826
845148LV00017B/679

* 9 7 8 1 4 2 5 5 8 9 8 9 9 *